ZEN
LIFE

AN OPEN-AT-RANDOM
BOOK OF GUIDANCE

DANIEL
LEVIN

ZEN
LIFE

AN OPEN-AT-RANDOM
BOOK OF GUIDANCE

DANIEL
LEVIN

st. lynn's
press

PITTSBURGH

Zen Life
An Open-at-Random Book of Guidance

ISBN-13: 978-0-9800288-7-4

Library of Congress Control Number: 2009924723
CIP information available upon request

First Edition, 2009

St. Lynn's Press . POB 18680 . Pittsburgh, PA 15236
412.466.0790 . www.stlynnspress.com

Typesetting & cover design—Holly Wensel, Network Printing Services
Laughing Buddha illustration—Sandra Bruce
Editor—Catherine Dees

Printed in the United States of America
on recycled paper 🌐

This title and all of St. Lynn's Press books may be purchased for educational, business, or sales promotional use. For information please write:
Special Markets Department . St. Lynn's Press . POB 18680 . Pittsburgh, PA 15236

10 9 8 7 6 5 4 3 2 1

INTRODUCTION

In Zen, stories are often told as a way to awaken the mind to a new way of seeing things. My hope is that the stories and sayings in this book will serve as a gentle jolt to remind you to practice what you already know.

I wrote *Zen Life* as much for myself as for you. I gathered the things I most needed to remember into this easily accessible book – sayings and stories that have touch me deeply, some from world-renowned teachers, some my own, and others from seemingly meaningless moments that stuck in my soul.

Open *Zen Life* anywhere. Read it slowly, a page at a time, and see what, if any, feelings emerge. If something comes to you from a story, it is yours. Sit with it a few moments and simply watch the thoughts and feelings that arise. Allow it to guide you, without judgment.

Or use it as a talisman: Meditate and ask for its guidance. It can help you to focus on a quality to remember for the day. Hopefully, it will speak to you as it does to me.

Wishing you unfathomable peace,

Danny

When you walk, walk.
When you sit, sit.

The goal of Zen
is to be totally aware in each moment.
Therefore, whatever you do,
do it with the totality of your being.
When you eat, eat.
When you sit, sit.
When you love, love.
This is Zen.

Be still

L et the world around you move.
The more it moves
the more it will return to where you are.
Take time to sit and watch life,
without action,
with only the stillness of your heart.
From this place
love all sentient beings,
pray for all to be free of suffering
and bless the planet with peace.

*Live
simply*

The more we have
the more we crave.
The less we have
the more we cherish all that we receive.
Live simply.
When we give things away
the universe fills us with something greater.

Share love

Sit with your eyes closed
and remember the last time you were loved completely,
unconditionally.
Linger in that feeling,
bathe yourself in unconditional love.
Now, expand it out through your whole body
to the room you are sitting in,
to the house, the neighborhood,
the city, the state, the country.
Keep expanding it out to embrace the continent,
the world, the planet, the galaxy, the universe.
Expand it until there is no place in creation
that is not touched by your love.
Now, take all of that love
and direct it to the one person in your life
who is the most troublesome,
and then to the one that you love the most deeply.

Chop wood,
carry water

Our spirituality
is not measured in how long we meditate
or how many hours we pray,
but in the simple way we live our lives –
in the way we chop wood,
in the way we carry water.
Allow each action you perform
to be a meditation.

*Live free from
all things*

There is a story they tell of a young boy
who while visiting the home of his teacher
breaks a very valuable cup.
When the teacher returns to the house
the boy cannot bring himself
to tell what happened.
The teacher looks at the boy and says,
"Everything in life has its moment:
It is born, it flourishes, and then it dies.
It is the natural course of things."
The boy brings the broken pieces
of the antique cup from behind his back,
and with tears in his eyes says he is sorry.
The teacher replies,
"That cup has served me well.
Serve all sentient beings, my son,
so that when it is your time to go,
all that remains
is the memory of the service you have done.

All things
are possible

Because something has not been done in the past
does not mean that in the future
it will never be done.
When you know there is something you must do,
do it.
No matter how many people have tried
and failed before you,
no matter how many times you yourself have tried and failed,
continue on.

Complete faith

Of all the lessons I have learned,
the greatest ones have come to me from my daughter.
Perhaps due to a developmental delay from birth,
the things of this world do not seem so important to her.
In times like this,
when the economy is broken
and it seems like the sky is falling,
I look to her for my guidance.
She lives with complete faith that everything she needs
will be given to her, and somehow it is.

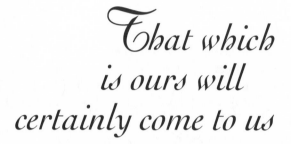

*That which
is ours will
certainly come to us*

We spend so much time worrying:
Is this the right person for me,
the right job,
the right house?
That which is ours is ours.
Similarly, that which is not ours is not ours.
Nothing we can do will ever change that.

*Rules kill
the spirit*

Be careful how many rules govern your life.
Though it is true
that rules help us to live an orderly life,
they also at the same time
eat away at the spirit of things.
Once in a while break the rules,
live 'outside the box,'
do something
no one ever would expect you to do.

*Practice kindness
without anyone
ever knowing*

Do things no one can trace.
Live life unrecognized,
slip money into the pocket of someone
without their knowing.
Become a miracle
by silently changing the lives of others.

*Believe
in who you
are*

Know that you are not the person you see,
not the face in the mirror
nor the body that carries you.
You are not your achievements
nor are you your shortcomings.
You are the light of the universe.
What is there not to believe in?

*In one moment,
everything in life changes*

Some time ago a friend asked me
why I was not in a relationship.
I answered that there simply was not enough time.
I was too busy
and did not have the space in my life for a relationship.
Two weeks later
I met someone and everything changed.
Now, not only was there time,
but it seemed that all I did was think about her.
In one moment everything changed.
And in another moment
it can and will change again.

Be compassion

A voice
just like that of yours and mine
spoke to me
from nowhere
and everywhere,
three times,
telling me to
"be compassion."
I did not understand.
I sat,
then realized
I was not being asked
to be compassionate,
but rather to let
the quality of compassion
breathe through me.

*Teach not with words,
but with
who you are*

The first sermon of the Buddha had no words.
There was no lofty perch upon which he stood,
no crowd of people awaiting his sermon.
The first teaching the Buddha gave
was the way he walked into the marketplace.
Upon seeing him and the way he moved,
people thought, I want to walk like him,
and they became his students.

Nothing is wrong

Walk slowly into teachings
that promise to make you a better person than you are.
Sounds strange, I know.
But most things in life
try to make us other than what we are:
the relationships we have,
the jobs we do,
the religions we enter into.
Isn't the promise to make us better
also a subtle way of telling us we are not okay?
What would happen if we started from the thought that
nothing is wrong.
Try that on for the day and see how it feels.

Love everyone

A friend was worried about her finances.
I suggested to her
that she think less about money
and more about how she could help people
get exactly what they need.
I truly believe
that when we want the best for others
with no thought of self,
everything in life comes to us.
It is a law of the universe.
What we sow is what we reap.
Give for the sheer pleasure of giving.

Happiness comes from within

If we build our happiness
on the things around us,
one day for sure
we will lose our happiness.
For all things in this world are ephemeral,
here today, gone tomorrow.
Why then be happy when we have things
and sad when we do not?
Find that happiness
that can never be taken from you.

Be here now

This moment
is the only real thing that exists.
Win the moment
and the hours, days and years will be yours.

Everything passes

The sun rises,
the sun sets.
We are born,
we die.
We live our lives
as if we will be here forever.
yet, we have no idea how long we have on this earth.
All we know for sure
is that one day our time here will pass.
Therefore, live each moment as if it were your last.

*May all beings
know happiness
and avoid suffering*

All of us want the same thing,
to find happiness
and avoid suffering.
The way to do this is to find contentment
in where life has placed you.
Suffering comes from wanting things
to be different than they are.
Happiness comes
from accepting what is.

Set down the things
that burden you

Two monks
(who had taken a vow to never touch a woman)
were walking, when they came to a fast flowing river.
As they started to cross,
a young woman standing at the river's edge
asked if they would help her cross too.
The first monk said, "Absolutely not,"
and started across the river.
The second monk simply picked her up and carried her,
after which he set her down and continued on his way.
Five miles later, the first monk,
who had been quietly fuming all this time,
said to the second monk,
"How could you possibly have done that?
We have both taken a vow to never touch a woman."
The second monk replied,
"Brother, I picked her up, carried her to the other side
and set her down again.
But you have been carrying her for the last five miles."
Do what you need to do and then let it go.

Be yourself

Why spend time worrying
about whether people like you or not?
People are wrong so much of the time.
If they like you they could be wrong,
and if they don't like you they could be wrong.
So why worry about what they think of you?
What is important is what you think about yourself.

*Do what no one
has done before*

The Rebbe used to say to me,
"When there is no man, you be the man."
Rather than waiting for someone else to do something
and wondering why no one does it,
you do it.
While others vie to be important,
practice unimportance.
Serve all beings with compassion.

We are one

Within a very short period of time
every molecule in our body changes.
We breathe in new molecules
and exhale others that have been within us.
In the very air we breathe exist
the molecules of Hitler, Stalin and Mussolini.
And in that same inhalation
are also the molecules of Buddha, Gandhi and Jesus.

Courage

Several years ago, traveling,
I came upon the place
where revolutionaries risked everything they had
and dumped British tea into the water.
Sounds like nothing to us now,
this little Tea Party in Boston Harbor,
but tea was an essential part of the British culture
and this was a deeply symbolic act.
I sat there and thought about the courage it took
to do what they had done.
As I sat longer,
I wondered if I might have the courage to do such a thing.
And then it struck me:
Did I have the courage now
to take everything I believed in
and dump it over the sides of my own mind?
I sat for hours,
mentally throwing everything I was
into that water.
Challenge all that you believe.
A belief is just a belief, it is not a fact.

The last 10%

The teacher sat with her students
and spoke to them of change.
Each of them was so happy
with the progress they had made.
She said, "You are right to feel happy.
To change oneself is hard,
but remember, it is easier to change the first 90% of yourself
than it is to change the remaining 10%,
for that last 10% is who you think you are."
Look at that part of yourself you are holding onto:
Is that really who you are?

*Know what is you
and what is not*

The student came to the teacher saying,
"I feel terrible about myself.
I have an awful temper.
Do you have any idea how I can heal it?"
"You have something very strange, indeed," said the teacher.
"Let me see it right now."
"But I cannot show it to you in this moment," said the student,
"It comes when it comes
and goes when it goes."
"Then it must not be your true nature," the teacher said.
"If it were, you could show it to me at any time.
Your true nature is that which always is."

Practice
non-judgment

Once there were four very good friends
who decided to enter the monastery together.
They took a vow of silence
so that they could absorb themselves in stillness.
The first day came and went without a sound.
On the eve of the second day,
their lamps ran out of oil
and the first monk said to the servant,
"Fix the lamps."
The second monk, shocked, looked to the first and said,
"We are not supposed to say a word."
The third scolded the other two, saying,
"You both are stupid. Why did you talk?"
The fourth monk sat proudly and then said,
"I am the only one who has not spoken."
That which we judge stands in the way
of that which we aspire to be.

Center everywhere

All spiritual teachings
teach people how to live
more from their center.
But what would happen if our center was everywhere?
Try to feel yourself a part of all sentient beings.
How would you treat them now?

*Who you are
speaks louder
than what you say*

He had devoted his whole life to the study of Zen
and was known through the land as a holy man.
One day, his relatives came seeking his guidance.
One of their sons was squandering
the family's fortune, spending it on courtesans
and placing the family in danger of losing everything.
So the holy man, now up in years,
traveled many miles to see the boy.
When he arrived at the house,
it was already late and he retired immediately.
All through the night, the holy man sat in meditation.
In the morning, after breakfast, he prepared to depart,
saying to his young host,
"I must be getting old, my hands shake now.
Would you be so kind as to help me tie the string of my sandals?"
The young man did so.
Upon which the holy man simply said,
"You see, a man becomes older and feebler day by day.
Please take good care of yourself."
He never said a word about the courtesans
or the complaints of the boy's relatives.
Yet from that moment on,
the boy stopped living as he had.

Act without effort

D o those things in life that are effortless
and joy will be yours.
This does not mean
to avoid things that are hard,
but rather, to relax
and find ways to make
what is hard soft,
what is difficult easy,
what is undoable done.

Enjoy the moment

She was going on pilgrimage to India,
to get away from it all,
to concentrate and focus only on her practice.
But for the months preceding her visit,
she worried about everything
as she was new to travel
and uncertain how she would deal
with the rigors of being in a country
so different from her own.
Hesitation and excitement flooded her being,
and there were times
when she almost called the whole thing off.
But once she arrived, something wonderful happened:
Her spirit relaxed into the vibration of the land,
and though there were certainly moments of concern,
she found that all the things she had worried about
melted away and became as nothing.
So often, what we worry about never materializes.

Better late than never

He started his practice of Zen at the age of 60.
By the time he was 80, he was world-renowned
as someone who had reached enlightenment,
and people from across the land sought his counsel.
He taught for 40 more years
until he retreated to the mountains.
It's never too late to start something
you have always wanted to do.

*Walk life
without leaving
footprints*

Tread lightly on this earth.
　　Be like the wind,
touching others
without any thought of recognition.
The wind just blows.
Rather than leaving footprints,
it erases them.
Walk in this way
without a sense of ego.
Become more invisible.

*The laws of
the universe are bigger
than the laws of the day*

It was a time of famine in the village.
The people here were no strangers to suffering.
They had always pulled together to survive,
but these times were harder,
and the people had lost their spirit.
Now, instead of thinking how to help each other,
all they could think of was their own survival.
They went to the teacher and asked his counsel.
The teacher said simply, "The laws of the universe
are bigger than the laws of the moment.
When you give to the world
the world is obliged to give back to you.
Therefore, in times like these
give to one another,
not with the thought of what you will get back,
but rather with the desire to love more completely.
In doing so,
you will be paving your own temple with bricks of gold.
This time will pass, and when it does
you will all be stronger."

What you think today, you become tomorrow

Watch your thoughts throughout the day and you will see the map of your future staring back at you.

*Just as
we are*

The two students of Zen sat together
and spoke of the challenges of love and life.
Each opened herself up to the other
and the discussion soon came to focus on relationships.
"Why do they start out so wonderfully," one asked,
"and then become so hard?"
The other thought a while and replied,
"As time goes on,
the reality of who the other person is
overcomes the fantasy of who we thought they were.
The problems arise when we try to change them
into who we want them to be."
The first student smiled in agreement and said,
"What would happen
if we loved and accepted each other just as we are?"

Two
bags

The teacher set two bags on the table.
Each bag held both the joys and sorrows
of the lives of the boys in front of them.
She told them,
"Choose the bag you want to take home with you."
Both chose their own bag.
The teacher then said,
"Remember this when you feel that life is too hard.
Given the chance to trade your life for that of another,
you chose your own bag of life."

Avoid suffering,
be happy

It sounds so easy, maybe it is:
Stop doing the things that bring pain.
Start doing the things that bring happiness.

*One never knows
what the day brings*

They had grown up together, the best of friends.
Time had separated them,
but today they sat and spoke
of the joys and hardships of their separate lives.
One had chosen the way of spirit,
going to the mountaintop to sit at the feet of his teacher,
while the other had chosen the way of the world
and become a businessman.
Both had achieved great success in their chosen paths.
When each spoke, the other listened with rapt attention.
As the day drew to a close,
the monastic asked his friend for a donation to the monastery.
The businessman smiled and said,
"You, my long lost friend, have hit the jackpot today.
The doctors tell me I have an incurable disease
and I will in all likelihood be dead within the year.
All that I have I give to you and the monks in your hermitage."
Tears came to the monk's eyes
and he touched his friend on the forehead,
the illness now gone forever.
They wept for the selfless love they shared.
For the rest of the day they roamed the streets of the village,
drunk with the joy of all that had happened
By evening, they were on their way to the mountaintop
to live a life of solitude – together.

The
cageless
bird

For many years, the bird lived in his cage.
One day his cage was left open
and now he was free
to fly through the whole house.
But the bird would not come out.
He had grown so used to the cage,
he did not feel safe outside of it.
In what places in our lives is the gate to our cage open,
yet we remain bound and do not fly?

Remember

In India, there is a sign on their highways that says
"Avoid Accidents"
I always wondered
why would they write something so obvious,
and then I realized,
we are often not shown things we need to learn,
but rather things we need to remember.
Then it all made sense.
Avoid accidents.

*What we see is
who we are*

There is a story they tell of two dogs.
Both at separate times
walk into the same room.
One comes out wagging his tail
while the other comes out growling.
A woman watching this
goes into the room to see
what could possibly make one dog so happy
and the other so mad.
To her surprise
she finds a room filled with mirrors.
The happy dog found
a thousand happy dogs looking back at him
while the angry dog
saw only angry dogs growling back at him.
What you see in the world around you
is a reflection of who you are.

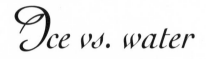

Ice vs. water

The teacher came
and changed the lives of millions of people.
When he died,
the students, in their desire to be true to his teaching,
kept everything just as it was when he was alive.
They did just as he had always done
and did not change a thing.
Over time, his spirit – which was free-flowing like water –
became solid like frozen ice.
In trying so hard to keep the essence of who he was
they lost the very thing that made him great, his fluidity.

Practice
cooperation

There is a story they tell that when we leave this world,
our arms become stiff and do not bend.
In the place they call hell
everyone suffers from starvation
because they are unable to feed themselves.
In the place they call heaven
no one starves,
because here everyone feeds each other.

What changed?

They lived a distance apart, but one day they met,
and the moment they did
something happened.
Both experienced a love deep love
that had not been known before.
Their hearts, minds, souls and bodies became one.
How they looked,
where they lived,
how much money they had – all became irrelevant.
But, as time passed, the distance between them grew painful.
Their limited finances
made it impossible for them to see each other often,
and they now longed for something they once had
but had no more.
The pain consumed them until it became unbearable.
One moment, all they knew was love.
The next, all they knew was pain.
What changed?

Who is
dreaming what?

A sage went to sleep one night
and dreamt he was a butterfly,
only to be awakened by a sudden noise.
When he opened his eyes, he questioned,
"Am I a man, dreaming I was a butterfly,
or am I a butterfly dreaming I am a man?"
Who are you in reality?

Flip of a coin

Never in their memory had things gotten so bad.
The economy was spiraling out of control
and a paralyzing fear gripped the people.
They asked the revered teacher of the nearby monastery
what the future held and what they should do.
To their dismay, he said, "I have no idea.
I have never seen a time like this.
And so I will do something I have never done before:
I will flip a coin and put our future into the hands of fate.
If the coin comes up heads, we will prosper.
We will have to take risks now, but they will pay off.
If the coin comes up tails, we will not prevail.
The times will swallow us up and we will crumble."
He tossed the coin high in the air
while everyone watched, expectantly.
A cheer went up as the coin landed...on heads.
With confidence in the future,
the people started in a new direction.
It was not long before the land prospered again.
When asked how he could have risked so much
on the toss of a coin,
the teacher held it up to show that it was heads on both sides.
What we believe is what we create.

*The same
but different*

Why, in water,
does everything weigh less
than on dry land?
Learn the way of the water
and things will not be heavy.

*No one
can take
anything
from you*

While the abbot was reciting his prayers,
a thief with a sharp sword entered his room.
Without turning around the abbot said,
"What you seek is in that drawer.
I do not have time to be bothered by you."
The thief started to take what was in the drawer,
when the abbot said,
"Do not take it all, I have to buy food today."
The thief put some back.
As he turned to leave, the abbot spoke again, saying,
"When you receive a gift, say thank you."
The thief thanked him and left.
Months later, the thief was caught and tried in court.
The abbot was called as a witness to testify against him,
but when he was questioned, answered,
"This man did not steal anything from me.
He came into my room, I gave him a gift
and he thanked me for it."
When the thief got out of jail,
he returned to the abbot and became his devoted student.

Let your light shine

Have you ever noticed
how bright even the smallest light looks
when everything outside is dark?
In turbulent times,
share your light.
No matter how little you think you have
it will shine bright.

*Let go of the things
that are hard*

As I get older,
I see life with a different set of eyes.
Many things that were once so important to me
are simply not that important anymore.
Here is one thing I have learned:
Things come and go in life
to help us change.
Once the moment of change comes,
we must let the situation go.
If we resist,
the situation will completely drain us.
It is not easy to let go,
but it is much more painful
to try to hold on to something that wants to pass.
Therefore, practice the path of least resistance.
Do that which is easy
and let go of that which is hard.

Inside, we are all the same

Two people.
One practices religion,
one does not.
Still, both are children of God.
Outward appearances only highlight our differences.
Look behind the trappings of race, religion and pedigree
to see we are all the same.

*Treat all
as if they were
a holy man*

Word had spread across the land
that a holy man had come to live in the small house
at the top of the mountain.
People from far and wide made the trek to see him.
An elderly man from the neighboring village
decided he too would make the difficult journey
up the mountain.
When he arrived, he said to the servant at the door,
"I have come to see the holy man."
The servant showed him around the house
and then led him out the back door.
The old man shouted, "Why do you lead me out?
I have come to see the holy man!"
"You already have," replied the servant and shut the door.
See the holy man everywhere,
especially in people
with whom you are having the most problems.

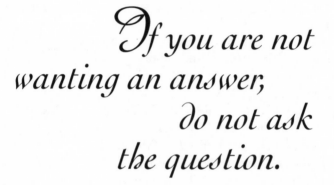

*If you are not
wanting an answer,
do not ask
the question.*

They came to her to ask questions,
for she was able to see things most could not see.
But sometimes when she answered,
they fought her, resisting what she had to tell them.
"Why ask me your questions," she said,
"if you are unwilling to hear answers?
You are like a deaf person.
Do not ask if you cannot hear."

The
forgetting saint

The monk was asked to come to the village,
as the people were struggling through great hardships.
He was soon surrounded by villagers
urgent to ask him questions.
One by one they rose,
but as soon as they stood in front of him
they could no longer remember their questions.
He sat and waited.
When no one said anything, he got up to leave.
The moment he left, all the people's questions returned.
What happened?
In his presence
their energy had been raised to a place
where their problems no longer existed.
Live above your problems.

Who are you?

清和
宗永

They say there are three ways you can tell
who a person really is:
the way people are when they drink,
how they become when they are angry,
and the way they spend their money.
What do these three actions
tell you about yourself?

*You never know
what is around
the corner*

His business had done incredibly well in its first three years, doubling in sales every year.
All signs pointed to continued success.
Based on the company's projected growth,
he hired more staff,
moved to an office that could accommodate them
and put ambitious programs into place.
And then, like a tsunami, the bottom fell out of the economy.
He stood on the brink of losing everything,
yet he did not appear to be in despair.
A local from the town came to his office and said,
"With everything going on, you still seem so positive.
How can that be?"
The owner responded, "All of this is not who I am.
What does despair do to help anything?
I may have lost my business, but that does not mean
I have to lose my happiness as well."

*It is all
so simple*

I was just telling a friend of mine about my daughter.
She has a developmental delay
and does not relate to the things of this world
in the way that the rest of us do.
"There is something beautiful about her," I said.
"When she is hungry she eats,
when she is tired she sleeps."
This morning, I came upon this Zen story
and had to laugh:
A student comes to his teacher and asks,
"What is enlightenment?"
The teacher replies,
"When hungry, eat.
When tired, sleep."

One God

The same God that watches over us
when times are great
watches over us
when they are not.

Receive

He came to the temple to offer his services.
Times were hard,
and since he had a gift for finances
he wanted to help the temple get back on its feet.
After several weeks
the abbot wished to repay him for his efforts,
but every time he offered to do something for the man,
the man changed the subject.
Finally, the abbot looked him in the eye and said,
"You don't need to do things for me in order for me to like you.
I liked you the moment I saw you."
The man cried, because all his life
he had harbored the belief that people would not like him
if he did not do things for them.
In that moment
he learned to receive.

*One thing
we all
share*

All of us want
to love
and be loved.
It is that simple.

Burn slowly

The mistake I make
again and again and again
is that when I feel something I race towards it.
I am a very passionate man
and so when that passion is lit,
the spark turns into a raging fire.
I always thought that was one of my best qualities:
no hesitation.
But as I reflect back on life
I often find that the fire that rages
burns quickly and then dies,
while the fire that burns slowly remains.

Only one love

He came to his teacher in tears.
He had spent his whole life caring for others,
and giving everything he had to help them.
Now, all that he had was gone,
and many of those he had helped no longer spoke to him.
He wondered aloud what had gone wrong.
His teacher, a woman of great wisdom,
took his hands and said,
"Everything in this world will one day disappoint you.
There is only one love that will never vanish:
the love of God.
You can love God or not love God,
he will always love you.
You can treat him well or not treat him well,
he will always love you.
You can honor him or betray him,
he will always love you.
Give your love to him now
and your sorrow will be gone.

The way
of
grace

If we need to change
and we do not do it on our own,
oftentimes the world steps in
and does whatever it must
to make the change happen.
One way invites grace,
the other does not.
Choose the way of graceful change.
Do what needs to be done.

The sheer joy
of giving

When I was a child
I remember saving up my money for months
to buy my brother a baseball glove and bat for the holidays.
When he opened my presents he was so happy,
they were just what he wanted.
He then handed me my present, a pack of baseball cards.
It wasn't fair. I said to him, "Give me my presents back!"
The thoughts of an immature child.
I wish I could say that over the course of my life
I learned from that lesson, but I cannot.
To this day, I still suffer at times
from this tit for tat way of thinking.
I need to be reminded that all we give
will one day be given back to us.
It is a law of karma.
But if we give with the thought
that we deserve something back,
we will suffer as I did that morning.

Day becomes night
night becomes day

There is nothing
we can do
to change the obvious flow of life.
Trying to stop the day from becoming night
is as senseless as trying to stop the changes
that are happening in our lives.

Talking
with God

The student was so excited.
In meditation she had been praying for an answer
to what she should do with her life.
Suddenly, she heard the answer loud and clear.
She got up and ran off in the direction she was given.
At first it all seemed effortless,
but it became harder and harder,
so difficult that finally she could not go on.
She went back into meditation,
praying again for an answer.
And once again the voice of her teacher came saying,
"Yes indeed, I did tell you to turn left, but only for one block.
Then I wanted you to turn right.
But in your zeal,
you did not listen to the full message
and went left forever."

One or the other

He came to the teacher,
already a student of another teacher, saying,
"I want to learn from you."
The teacher said, "Then leave your other teacher."
The boy, confused by this response, said,
"But I want to learn from you how to sit,
and from her how to move."
The teacher replied,
"Already in the first moments
you have not done as I have requested.
How can I teach you?"
Trying to catch two rabbits, you catch neither.

Cold and warm

When it is cold outside
we put on many layers of clothing to protect ourselves.
When we are cold to others
they put on many layers of protection too.
But when it is warm outside, less protection is needed.
To touch others, be warm.

Reflections

He looked around and saw that his life was in shambles. His business, his romantic relationship, his family – everything.
He began to see that the disarray of the world around him was merely a reflection of his own life.
His house was out of order.
So he spent his days now at home,
polishing his mirror,
changing his way of seeing,
hoping that when he went out into the world again,
the reflection he saw would be different.
What we see is who we are.

Angels among us

He walked into my shop to buy clothes for his wife.
We were having a Grand Opening
Going Out of Business sale.
The man made a purchase and went home,
only to return the next day.
His wife had loved the clothes.
He wanted to see if there was something he could do
to help us pull out of the current situation.
He asked for no money, nor did he seek any other reward.
He simply wanted to help us.
I opened myself to him and we have become friends.
Will the business be able to be saved?
Time will tell. In the meantime,
I met have someone who has completely touched my heart
and has become a friend.
Isn't life amazing?
In the pit of despair, angels come!

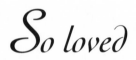
So loved

Much of his life he had spent helping others.
It was his nature to do so.
When hard times struck and he was down,
many people reached out to him
from directions he had never anticipated.
The help he had given others
was now being returned a thousand-fold.
He realized in that moment
just how love worked,
as if for the first time in his life.

Perhaps

The monks at the monastery were in charge of the horses.
One day, one of the horses ran away
The monks came to the abbot and told him of their bad luck
and his great misfortune.
The abbot replied only, "Perhaps."
The next day,
the horse returned,
along with three handsome wild stallions.
The monks told the abbot of his now good fortune.
His reply again was, "Perhaps."
The next day,
a young apprentice climbed atop one of the stallions
and was thrown to the ground with a broken leg.
The monks reported the unfortunate news,
and the abbot replied only, "Perhaps."
The very next day,
when the military came to draft the young boys for war,
the apprentice with the broken leg was passed by.
The monks came again to the abbot to tell him the good news.
This time all the monks and the abbot together said, "Perhaps."
Do your best to not get caught up in the emotions of the moment.

New
beginnings

As the roots of a growing tree
push up through the ground,
the plants and bushes
that were once nearby
are pushed aside to make room.
Often the way of nature is the way of this world.
When we find our lives are being torn apart,
look to see if the roots of a new beginning
are growing within.
Make room for that which is coming.

Crossing the river brings good fortune

Do what you have been longing to do.
Know that whatever happens
you are blessed.
Hesitate no more.
This is the moment to make your move.

Look pain
in the eye

I had been hurt.
Several of the relationships in my life had changed.
The way I chose to protect myself
was to put up psychic walls
so that no one could get in.
This caused more pain,
which made me shut down even more.
The walls I built now became my prison.
I had to break out.
To experience joy again
I had to push through this pain.
It took all the courage I had
to look that pain in the eye
and walk through it.

Be kind to all

He had been well known, but as happens in life,
his mercurial ride took him up,
only to drop him down,
then raise him higher up than ever before.
I watched the people around him.
befriend him when he was up,
and leave him when he was down.
To his glory, he was unfazed by how people treated him,
but it struck me:
Rare is that human being who is respectful to everyone
no matter what their station in life.

The eyes of others
often see
more clearly

Sometimes what others see in us
is more true than what we see in ourselves.
Therefore, listen to their praise and their criticism
with an open heart.
If what they say is true, bless them for helping you
to see something you were not able to see.
If what they say is not true,
drop it in the first trash can you find.

Live now

The business started from a fire in the pit of his stomach
that wouldn't let him go.
It was something he had to do.
The more he pushed it away,
the more it consumed him
until he could think of nothing else
but building it into an empire for his children to inherit.
A friend said to him one day,
"I have been watching you. Are you sick?"
"No, why do you think that?" he replied.
"Because of the way you are behaving.
It seems to me that you are building your business
as if you are getting ready to die.
But you are a young man, a seemingly long way from death.
Why not do business as you did in the beginning,
for the sheer joy
of creating beautiful things
and serving others?"
So often the present gets lost in preparation for the future.
Live now.

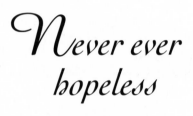

*Never ever
hopeless*

She could see no way out.
In her mind,
there was nothing anyone could do to help her.
So she sat crippled by her thoughts, wanting to give up.
From a thousand miles away
I could easily see the source of her pain:
The thoughts she was thinking were manifesting in her life.
What was much harder for me to see
was that my own situation was virtually the same.
Though I never contemplated giving up,
my thoughts, too, were creating the uncomfortable reality
I was choosing to live in.
Changing our thoughts can change our lives.

*What you give,
you receive*

The student came to the teacher and asked,
"How do I prepare myself
for the teaching you are about to share?"
The teacher replied, "Think of me as a bell:
A gentle tap will produce a soft ring,
whereas a strong tap will make the bell sing.
The more you are willing to give of yourself
the more you will receive."

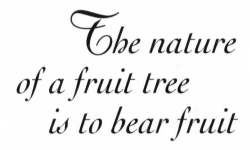

*The nature
of a fruit tree
is to bear fruit*

We sat together, she and I, and talked about life.
She had recently returned to her hometown
where old friends had gathered to see her.
One man stood up and said of her,
"No matter what happens to you, you are always the same.
Fame and fortune have not changed you, nor hard times.
You have always loved without condition
and trusted everyone."
As she told me this,
she lamented that perhaps she trusted too much
and had been hurt too many times because of it.
I said to her,
"I know the pain that trusting others has caused you,
but you can do nothing else.
It is the nature of a fruit tree to bear fruit."
In that moment, I realized that without intending it,
she was teaching me the lesson I most needed to learn.

A teacher teaches

One of the monks in the temple
was found stealing from the others.
After being confronted and talked to,
he promised he would never do it again.
But several weeks later, he stole once more.
The monks came to the abbot,
demanding that the thieving monk
be forced to leave the temple,
or else they themselves would leave.
The abbot looked at the aggrieved faces and said,
"All of you know right from wrong,
therefore, if you need to go, go.
This young monk does not know the difference,
so he will remain here with me.
It is my obligation to be with him until he learns."
The monks cried upon seeing their lack of compassion,
and the "stealing monk" never stole again.

*Courage
amidst
crashing
worlds*

The village was being destroyed by a rival army.
Everyone fled but the abbot of the temple.
Upon hearing that this old, peculiar man was still there
the general of the rival army demanded to see him.
As the abbot approached, the general said to him,
"What kind of fool are you to act so defiant?
Do you not realize you are standing before a man
who could run a sword through you
without even blinking an eye?"
To which the abbot responded,
"And do you realize that you are standing before a man
who could have a sword run through him
without blinking an eye?"
How do we develop the courage
to know in our hearts, not just our minds,
that nothing in this world can ever harm us?

Change not my circumstances, change me

A very saintly woman once said,
"The things that happen to us do not matter.
What we become through them
is all that is important."
When we live in this way,
we find peace.

*Expect
nothing*

When we expect something
we set ourselves up for unhappiness.
The wise person lives expecting nothing from life
and giving everything to it.
In this way
sadness vanishes
and happiness thrives.

*Our words
have power*

The monastery practiced silence,
but one day a year the monks were allowed to speak,
to share their gratitude with one another.
But towards the end of that day,
one after the other began to speak of hurts
done to them by others.
Little pains had become big scars
because no one was able to speak about them.
But now, with speaking,
things were working themselves out.
Observing this, the abbot said,
"We have been an order that practices silence and prayer.
Yet, today I have seen how past hurts
are nurtured silently in our hearts,
and prayers alone have been unable
to set things right between us.
I have also seen how long standing pains
have been resolved in minutes.
Therefore, from today on, we will no longer practice silence.
Our words have the power to hurt or heal.
Use them, as you have today,
to heal yourselves and the world."

Go deeper

I remember the first day I was in the Holy Land,
the feelings of tremendous joy and overwhelming pain.
On the surface, the land was at war and people were suffering,
but underneath were layers of history, civilization
and the footsteps of saints whose vibrations were still there,
permeating everything.
It took me by complete surprise, how this could be.
And then I thought about my life and realized…
outwardly, there has been much pain
yet inwardly, so much joy.
Remember the Holy Land.
Look beneath the surface of life and see where joy dwells.

The monk walked into a room
where philosophers were debating
the existence of a holy man
who was said to have lived many years ago.
There were those who believed in his existence
and those who did not,
saying it was merely stories made up
to teach others how to live.
In the middle of the debate
the monk stood up and simply said,
"I have seen him," and then walked out.
The debate was over.
Do not believe because others have believed before you
or because they say it is the right thing to do.
Do not believe because people around you pressure you
or even because it makes you feel better to do so.
Believe because you have experienced.
That belief is unshakable.

Go to the center

In Zen,
the answer always lies
in being more centered.
That is where everything blossoms.
The more we stay at the periphery,
the more we are spun out as the wheel of life turns.
But when we get to the center,
we ride the turn of the wheel without tension.

*The waves come in,
the waves go out*

Everything in life changes,
yet we think what is now
will always be.
It will not.
Just as the waves ebb and flow,
so will all situations in life come and go.

Growing
tomatoes

For my birthday,
my best friend gave me a garden box
and two tomato plants.
I planted them in the box, gave them good soil
and watered them every day.
After a while, one plant started producing lots of tomatoes,
while the other grew more slowly
and had yellowed leaves.
I loved both of those plants.
Through them, I saw the way of the divine:
Some of her children produce a lot of fruit,
some produce a little.
Some have problems,
others do not.
But the love of the divine for her children never falters.
No matter what you have done or not done,
know that you are loved completely,
just because you are you.

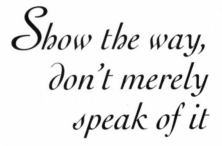

Show the way,
don't merely
speak of it

The ruler of the land was a humble man
and a longtime student of Zen.
He came every day to sit with his teacher.
Never did his exalted position interfere with his discipleship.
One day, the ruler asked the teacher,
"What is egotism?"
The teacher replied in a very condescending way,
"What kind of stupid question is that?
You have studied with me all these years,
and can ask a stupid question like that?"
This answer so shocked the ruler
that he became angry and defensive.
The teacher smiled and said,
"That, my king, is egotism."

Green flash

They sat watching the sun as it set into the ocean.
The day was clear and cloudless.
In the seconds before the sun set
there was a green flash of light on the horizon.
It is rare to see this, few ever do.
When everything is just right, it happens.
Live life like this…
so that when you breathe your last breath here on earth,
the world lights up.

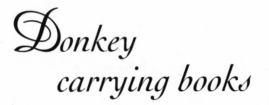

Donkey carrying books

So often we understand things with our heads,
but are unable to live it in our hearts.
This is not real understanding.
And yet, so often we teach others from this place,
thinking we understand.
For me, real understanding comes
when I live what I know.
That is why I write these things as reminders to myself,
rather than as teachings to you.
For too many years,
I have been a donkey carrying books,
teaching things I did not did not fully understand.
Now, I hope together we can remind each other
of that which we value.
And help each other to be ourselves.

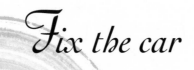
Fix the car

The other day
I rear-ended another car.
As soon as I got home
I called my insurance company
and arranged to have the car fixed.
It felt good.
I wonder why
when my body aches
I do not treat it with the same respect
I have for my car.

*Be like
the tree*

The tree grows leaves in the spring
and loses them in the fall.
But first, the leaves change color
and become more beautiful –
more radiant and 'alive.'
Then they effortlessly fall from the tree.
How different they are from us:
We too create something beautiful,
yet how many of us can let go of our creation
as effortlessly as that leaf falls.
Before going to sleep each evening
offer all that you have back into the hands of the creator.

*The clock
ticks*

The hands on the clock move forward,
never pausing to reflect
whether the moment that passed was good or bad,
never thinking whether it has the strength to go on.
It simply moves from moment to moment.
Be like the clock.
Go forward.

Everything matters, nothing matters

One day people may love you,
the next they might hate you.
In the end,
neither their praise
nor their blame matters.
What matters only is the goodness of your heart.

No
expectations,
no
disappointments

I went to a conference in a new city
to sell clothes I make
under my company name, ZENsei.
I was hoping to sell out of everything I'd brought.
As it happened,
only half the expected number of people attended
and sales were slow.
At first I was discouraged,
until I realized that a lot of people
who had never heard of ZENsei before,
now had bought my clothing.
Why let a false expectation
ruin a beautiful reality?

*Life is
a movie*

When we go to a movie
we forget that the people we are watching are actors,
playing roles to tell a story.
In the movie of our life we do the same thing:
We forget that the people we come in contact with are actors too,
handpicked to deliver the messages we most need to hear.

Wisdom

To help someone in the short run,
only to hurt them in the long run
is not an act of kindness.
To hurt someone in the short run
in order to help them in the long run shows integrity.
But to find a way to truly help people
without hurting them at all is wisdom.

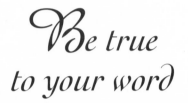

*Be true
to your word*

When you are true to your word,
people respect you.
More importantly,
you respect yourself.

Everything happens for a reason

When things happen,
  see the guiding hand behind it.
Why blame yourself
for all the things you could have done?
What happened, happened!
When we really understand
that God is the doer,
that is the moment we will feel peace.

Filling the hole

When things are taken from us,
it is often because
room needs to be created
for something new to enter.
If we only choose to see the hole,
we will miss the chance
to see the opportunity that is coming.

Completion

ACKNOWLEDGMENTS

This book would not be possible without the insight and kindness of Paul Kelly, founder and owner of St. Lynn's Press. He is not only one of my best friends, but he is also one of my teachers. Thank you, Paul.

To Catherine Dees, a gifted and gracious editor, and to Holly Wensel, an intuitive designer and typesetter: It has been an honor to work with you.

Thank you to all my teachers. Some of you are well known, others I have only seen from the corner of my eye as I passed you on the street, but something in the way you walked changed me.

To you who hold this book now in your hands, I thank you.

And lastly, and perhaps most importantly, I want from the bottom of my heart to thank my daughter, Elisa. You have given me the greatest gift possible. You have taught me love. I only hope that one day you will know how much I love you. It is to you, my precious, that I dedicate this book.

ABOUT THE AUTHOR

Daniel is the author of *The Zen Book*, *The Zen Cards* and *The Zen Journal*. He embodies his philosophy of centered balance in ZENsei, his line of environmentally conscious, high-end activewear apparel. Daniel lives with his beautiful daughter, Elisa, and a big, gentle golden retriever named Buddha, a few blocks from the beach near San Diego.

To learn more about his books and his clothing collections, please visit: www.ZENsei.com.

There is a saying in India:
     "When we are born, the world celebrates and we cry.
When we die, the world cries and we celebrate."
Our time here is so short
and yet when we are immersed in life,
it all seems so important.
But in reality…
our celebration will not be
for those things which are temporary:
not for the joys or the sorrows,
the successes or the failures.
Those are all just blips on the screen of life.
Instead, we will celebrate
how much we have loved,
for that is all that matters.
Therefore, love completely.
Love unconditionally.
And when you think you have no more to give,
just love more.
This is the ZEN life.